30 Days of Inspiration for...

Dew Drops

R. Martin

Introduction

Dear sisters in Christ—
May God bless you wherever you serve.
Thanks to all who helped bring this booklet into being.
All honor is the Lord's.
   -R. Martin

"The aged women likewise, that they be...teachers of good things; That they may teach the young women to be sober, to love their husbands, to love their children, To be discreet, chaste, keepers at home, good, obedient to their own husbands, that the word of God be not blasphemed" (Titus 2:3-5).

© Carlisle Press 2014 All Rights Reserved
All rights reserved. No portion of this book may be reproduced by any means, electronic or mechanical, including photocopying, recording, or by any information storage retrieval system, without written permission of the copyright owner, except for the inclusion of brief quotations for a review.

ISBN: 978-1-93375339-3
Rebecca Martin
Book Design by: Lori Troyer
Printed in the USA by Carlisle Printing of Walnut Creek

Carlisle Press
WALNUT CREEK

2673 Township Road 421
Sugarcreek, Ohio 44681
phone | 800.852.4482

Table of Contents

Dust Changed to Light 2
Vanishing Point. 4
Keeping Pure. 6
Smoking Flax 8
Deep Yet Clear 10
He Ran for Joy. 12
Redeemable. 14
Continue in My Love. 16
Sore Amazed 18
Because Jesus Had a Mother 20
Thy Light Is Come 22
The Proper Mortar 24
What Is the World? 26
All Mine Are Thine 28
Called to Be Saints 30
Petitions at the Throne. 32
Rejoice 34
Different Kinds of Seeing 36
Pictures from the Eclipse. 38
He Knew the Cost 40
Not All Was Told 42
At Thy Word 44
The Way of His Will. 46
Part 1: Doubts Can Have a Purpose. 48
Part 2: The Substance. 50
Family Affection 52
Drawn to the Fire 54
False Humility. 56
He Wanted to See 58
Groan Not 60

Day 1

Dust Changed to Light

At first they knew where Trissy's new kittens were: between the molasses barrel and the horses' stalls. But the old cat didn't appreciate three-year-old Adam's and five-year-old Mary's curiosity. After the children had come peering and exclaiming once too often, Trissy's kittens disappeared. In vain, Mary and Adam canvassed the farm to find their new haunt.

One obvious place, however, had been proclaimed off-limits: the haymow. So the children begged, "Mother, could we go up there if you went along? We're pretty sure Trissy goes up there."

Mother thought it over. "We'll climb the stairs very quietly, then sit there still as a mouse. Maybe we'll hear the kittens mewing."

Eyes sparkling, the children sneaked up the stairway with Mother, taking up motionless posts on a hay bale in the dim dustiness of the mow.

Suddenly, forgetting her vow of silence, Mary cried, "See the sunlight, Mother!"

Mother turned, following Mary's pointing finger. Shafting down from a crack high up in the barn wall was a band of brilliant sunlight, setting ablaze millions of tiny dust motes where darkness had reigned minutes before.

"I suppose the sun doesn't reach that crack till nearly noon," Mother surmised.

Mary barely heard her. Balanced on tiptoe, she stretched her hands as if to grasp the light. "I can touch it!" she crowed. "I can touch the sunlight."

One of the most beautiful and moving prophecies is that which Matthew renders thus in 4:16: "The people which sat in darkness saw great light; and to them which sat in the region and shadow of death light has sprung up."

How was that prophecy fulfilled? John tells us in 1:4,9: "In him was life; and the life was the light of men. That was the true Light, which lighteth every man that cometh into the world." Jesus came, preaching the kingdom and declaring (John. 8:12): "I am the light of the world: he that followeth me shall not walk in darkness, but shall have the light of life."

Often He taught in parables. How homely were Christ's stories, drawn from the everyday of His times! Lost lambs—mustard seeds—a woman baking bread—nothing was too common for Him to illustrate.

Yet like humble dust motes suffused with sunlight, as these everyday stories fell from the divine lips they became vivid spiritual truths that penetrated to the hearts of His thirsty listeners.

Day 2

Vanishing Point

Esther wasn't sure whether to laugh or cry as she contemplated her students' art. Being new to this school, she didn't know what aspects of art the teachers before her had stressed. But one thing seemed painfully obvious: these children didn't understand perspective! In their drawings the walls and roofs of buildings joined at impossible angles. Objects in the foreground were smaller than those at a distance.

Esther decided it was time for a lesson in perspective. She posted two drawings, one with things improperly aligned and all awry; and the other with a perfect vanishing point on the horizon that caused all the angles to flow into it and represented faraway objects smaller than those in the foreground.

All in all, Esther and her pupils had a lively session. Nothing intrigued the children more than the concept of a vanishing point. Young though they were, they could see how a vanishing point anchors a drawing and brings order out of chaos.

It was probably in the early summer of AD 50 that the Apostle Paul arrived in Thessalonica and there planted one of the earliest churches. With joy the people received the Gospel. However, according to Acts 17:1–10, Paul had to leave in haste, for there were those who sought after his life.

At the first opportunity, Paul sent Timothy back to visit the struggling little church. We can gather from his letter how his heart yearned over these new believers, almost like a mother worrying over her young children. Were they standing firm? Were they resisting the tide of evil that surged around them in this pagan city?

What joy, when Timothy was able to report that the Thessalonians were remaining steadfast and united. Yet he also reported problems. There were things the Thessalonians did not understand, and this lack was bringing disorder to their spiritual life.

They needed a better sense of perspective. They needed to see the big picture of God's plan. What was the "vanishing point" that Paul presented to them in his letters, the anchor to ground their faith during the persecution they suffered?

It is something that we today need just as much as those Thessalonian Christians needed it in AD 52. Our perspective on life is incomplete without it. It is the great and blessed hope of Christ's second coming. Threaded through his encouragements and admonitions, Paul reminded the Thessalonians again and again of this hope. "For the Lord himself shall descend from heaven with a shout, with the voice of the archangel, and with the trump of God…"

Day 3

Keeping Pure

"**Please may I** wear my good shirt and trousers today?" begged five-year-old Lamar. "I want to look nice when Grandpa and Grandma come. They will have good clothes on too, I'm sure."

Mother looked at the wiry little boy, who had just tumbled out of bed. "You mean you want to put on your good clothes now already? But can you keep them clean until our company arrives?"

"I'll try," he promised earnestly. So he was allowed to put on his freshly ironed blue shirt and a clean pair of trousers without patches. A few drops of Lamar's breakfast did splatter on his shirt, but he hoped the spots were so small that Grandma wouldn't notice.

Far worse was what happened twenty minutes later. Running through the barnyard, Lamar took a flip and landed on his side. "Oh, my trousers," he moaned, scrambling to his feet. From the waistband down past the knee, one side was completely covered with dirt!

Frantically, Lamar attempted to wipe it off. First he used his hands. Then he grabbed a bunch of grass and scrubbed at the soiled fabric. That only made things worse, because the grass left stains.

There was only one thing left to do. Sniffling, Lamar went in to Mother. She did not scold; she understood his pain, and she found another good pair of trousers for him to wear on this special day of Grandpas' visit.

"And every man that hath this hope in him purifieth himself, even as he is pure" (1 John 3:3). What is the hope within us that makes us want to be clean and pure? It is the hope of Christ's second appearing; and the hope that "when he shall appear, we shall be like him" (1 John 3:2). We desire purity, "even as he is pure."

"Keep thyself pure," admonishes Paul in 1 Timothy 5:22. "Cleanse your hands, ye sinners; and purify your hearts, ye double-minded," James warns sternly in 4:8.

But how can we do this? we ask in despair. *Can I in my own power keep myself pure?* Ah, no; Jesus says in John 15:5, "Without me ye can do nothing."

In 1 Peter 1:22 we are told how we can be purified: "Seeing ye have purified your souls in obeying the truth through the Spirit…" Let the Spirit of Christ within us be the crystal fountain of purity that can present us "clean every whit" and "without spot or wrinkle" at the second appearing of our beloved Lord.

Day 4

Smoking Flax

"Today would be a perfect day to burn the pile of twigs and refuse that we raked up from the lawn," declared Alice to her 15-year-old daughter, Janet. "With a coating of snow on the ground, there won't be any danger of the fire spreading."

"But the pile is all covered with snow!" Janet protested. "How will we ever get a fire started?"

Alice was undaunted. "The snow is so fluffy, we'll just dust it off the pile. Things are bound to be dry underneath."

Armed with newspapers and matches, mother and daughter headed for the back yard. On her knees, Alice struck the match and held it to the crumpled newspapers, strategically placed next to the dry twigs. Swift flames flared up, devoured the paper—and died.

"The twigs weren't even blackened," Janet pointed out ruefully.

Alice made no reply. Already she was holding the second match to more newspapers. As if mocking her efforts, the wind blew out the flames almost before the paper was consumed.

"It's no use," was Janet's opinion by the time her mother had used all seven of the matches she'd brought. "We've managed nothing but a bit of smoke. Let's throw snow on it and go in where it's warm."

"Wait," came a voice from behind them just as Janet scooped up some snow to quench the wisp of smoke. Father had arrived on the scene. He knelt near the smoking twigs and blew on them. Hesitant flames sputtered, then nearly died as a gust of wind attacked them. Father moved to the left so that his body prevented the wind from reaching the flames. Slowly but surely, they rose ever higher, until they engulfed the pile with humming, crackling heat.

"Smoking flax will he not quench." Those were among the eloquent words used by the prophet as he sought to describe the future Messiah in Isaiah 42. Our love is often no better than "smoking flax." We know that Christians are to "love one another with a pure heart fervently;" and then we wonder why we cannot love our fellow man better? Why is our love so poor and feeble?

Jesus does not despise our efforts. Quietly, gently, He comes and fans our smoldering affection with the breath of His pure love. With His own body that hung on the cross, He shelters and encourages to life a purer, glowing love in our hearts. And finally our feeble "smoking flax" is consumed in the limitless furnace of God's perfect love.

Day 5

Deep Yet Clear

Newly moved to a cozy little home in the Blue Ridge Mountains, James and Dora were eager to explore the wilderness around them. One day they headed east, where a vast jumble of rocks led them ever upward.

"I hear the tinkle of falling water!" exclaimed Dora, pausing for breath on the rugged climb. Soon they saw the stream, a narrow cascade plummeting down from boulder to boulder.

"I'd like to find its source," James declared. Searching out precarious handholds and footholds, they climbed until at last they found the spring-fed pool from which the stream began.

Throwing himself down on the brink, James gazed into the pool. "This is deep!" he whispered in awe. "Very deep, and yet the water is crystal clear."

"O the depth of the riches both of the wisdom and knowledge of God! how unsearchable are his judgments, and his ways past finding out!" exclaimed Paul in adoration. That was towards the end of Romans 11, a chapter where he tackles the complicated issues of God's dealings with the Jewish nation.

It was as if Paul, weary of his weighty arguments, finally threw his hands in the air and simply declared God's ways unfathomable—past finding out.

Now we come to the last verse of Romans 11, a verse very like that deep, crystal-clear pool discovered by James and Dora. It is deep because it seeks to express the profundity of God; and yet it is crystal clear because its language is so simple. The words are all one-syllabic. Any first-grader could read them. Listen to the sublime cadence of this little doxology:

"For of him, and through him, and to him are all things."

Of Him are all things: God is the spring, the fountain, the eternal source. The universe, the plan of salvation—all emanates out of God.

Through Him are all things: Through Him, that is, through Jesus Christ, the world was created, and through Him the marvelous stream of grace flows to us, His creation.

To Him are all things: If all is of Him and through Him, it follows that all shall return again to God as the ultimate end in a glorious tide of praise. This is the climax of the chapter: "To him be glory for ever. Amen."

Are we sometimes caught up in trying to fathom and figure out God's ways? We would do well to follow Paul's example, and simply throw ourselves down on the brink of His infinity, not trying to figure things out, but simply losing ourselves in adoration.

Day 6

He Ran for Joy

"**My puppy and** your kitten should run a race," said little Joseph to his even smaller sister, Katie. "We want to see who can run the fastest."

So they drew a line in the dirt to serve as the starting line. They drew the finishing line a little way across the yard. Carefully, Joseph positioned his puppy, instructing Katie to put down her kitten right beside him. "When I let go of Fido," he explained, "you let go of Kitty. I'm going to count to ten. Okay—now run!"

Nothing happened. Fido and Kitty looked around in a confused way. Then Kitty mewed happily and climbed into Katie's lap. Fido licked Joseph's ear.

Joseph scolded, "That's no way to run a race." Then he had an idea. "I know what. Kitty and Fido would surely run if they were allowed to run to us. But how can we make them stay here at the starting line while you and I go over to the finishing line?"

That problem was solved when big brother Henry agreed to hang onto the pets until Joseph and Katie had positioned themselves at the finish. Again Joseph counted to ten, then very loudly shouted, "RUN!"

This time they ran. Of course the puppy and the kitten had no sense of competition, but each romped joyfully across into the waiting arms of its owner. The pets paid little attention to the argument over who had won.

"Let us run with patience the race that is set before us," the Hebrews writer says in 12:1. Certainly we need patience in the race of the Christian life. But what motivates us? What gives wings to our feet and oxygen to our heaving lungs as we strive?

The answer lies in our Lord's example, as given in the next verse of Hebrews 12: "...Who for the joy that was set before him endured the cross..." Jesus ran for the joy that was set before Him! Hard though the race may be, we too may run for joy.

And what is the source of our joy? Who is standing there on the finish line irresistibly drawing us onward? "I press toward the mark for the prize," writes Paul to the Philippians, "of the high calling of God in Christ Jesus."

Jesus Himself is our prize. He is the source of the joy that draws us on. "I count all things but loss for the excellency of the knowledge of Christ Jesus my Lord," Paul cries in that same third chapter to the Philippians.

Many years ago there was a time when the prophet Habakkuk trembled because he saw that the Chaldeans were about to invade Judah. He threw himself down before the Lord to find out what he should do. Back came the Lord's reply: "Write the vision, and make it plain...that he may run that readeth it" (Hab. 2:2). Yes, the vision of Jesus has been written and plainly set before us. Let us run with patience and joy towards Him. "Looking unto Jesus, the author and finisher of our faith, who for the joy that was set before him endured the cross..." (Heb. 12:2).

Day 7

Redeemable

On a trip to town, Keturah was surprised at how sharp-eyed her five-year-old daughter was. Little Ella helped all she could; at the checkout she unloaded groceries onto the counter almost as fast as her mother. But Ella noticed something that her mother did not. Once back home, she exclaimed in a bewildered way, "That other lady used play money to pay for her things!"

Keturah knit her brows. "Do you mean the lady who was in front of us at the checkout? I don't think so. Play money doesn't work to buy things."

"Well, she did use some real money," Ella acknowledged, "but there was some that looked funny too. It had pictures of peanut butter and macaroni and ketchup—"

Keturah chuckled. "She must have had some coupons, Ella."

"What are coupons?" came the five-year-old's quick question.

"Hmmm. Let me see whether I can find one." Grabbing a flyer, Keturah pointed to a coupon for canned vegetables. "See, you get fifty cents off corn and peas if you hand in this little piece of paper when you're paying."

"Ah," said Ella. "And what's that long word there?"

"Redeemable."

"What does that mean?"

"Well, I know what redeem means, but I don't know just how to explain it... One thing I know, it's what Jesus does for us," Keturah replied.

Redeem. It's a powerful word. A Thesaurus gives a whole paragraph of synonyms, all words with a liberating power: repurchase, retrieve, free, liberate, ransom, rescue, save, deliver, recover, reinstate, atone, recompense, fulfill, perform, satisfy...

Words will never be sufficient to describe what Christ did—and does—for the world. How woefully condemned and cursed was mankind, after the fall in the garden of Eden! Not only was man forever banished from heaven, but man's earthly life became a burden and a drudgery. Toil and tears... thistles and pain... sweat and worry... all came as a result of sin.

Yet all is redeemable. On the cross, Christ atoned for sin, opening the way for the sinner to be reinstated in the grace of God. And through faith in Him, even the daily drudgery can be redeemed and transformed. True, there is still pain in child-bearing, but through Christ, the pain is enlarged into a beautiful mother-love. True, toil and sweat are still the lot of man, but in Christ, hard work becomes educative and ennobling.

Redemption—what a blessed word! "Where sin abounded, grace did much more abound" (Rom. 5:20). "But now being made free from sin, and become servants to God, ye have your fruit unto holiness, and the end everlasting life" (Rom. 6:22).

Dew Drops {TWO}

Day 8

Continue in My Love

A ROLL OF thunder rumbled down the midnight sky. Elsie awoke and sighed. Because their granddaughter was staying with them for a few days, Elsie knew what was going to happen.

Sure enough, before the next thunderclap died away, the patter of small feet sounded in the hall. Throwing on her robe, Elsie said to her husband, "I'm going to her in the living room."

Tears streamed down Lucy's face as she sobbed, "G-grandma, I'm sc-scared."

Elsie steered her to the couch and they sat side by side, Grandma's arm securely around Lucy's shoulders. Lightning flashed on the other side of the drapes; thunder crashed and boomed.

Lucy's eyes found Grandma's in the gloom. "The storm doesn't matter so much when I can feel your love." She drew her closer, and as they sat thus, words from John 15 came to her: "Continue in my love."

That was Jesus, speaking to His disciples in the last solemn hours before His betrayal. "Stay in my love. Abide in my love." Were tenderer words ever spoken?

Earlier, in verse 4, He had said, "Abide in me." Now it was "Abide in my love." He is drawing us closer, opening His heart to us.

Can we begin to fathom His love? "As the Father hath loved me, so have I loved you" (v.9). Mysterious, awe-inspiring words! How can we comprehend the depths of the love God has for His Son? Its dimensions are greater than the universe.

Jesus was worthy of that love. We are most unworthy. Yet Jesus loves us with the same love that God loves Him!

Such love is worlds away from the paltry love of a grandma who sighs because she needs to lose a bit of sleep on account of a frightened little girl. Still, Lucy in the circle of Grandma's arms is a picture—poor though it may be—of God's children abiding in the love of Jesus.

"Abide in my love," He says. And how is that done? Not only did Jesus *tell* us how: "If ye keep my commandments, ye shall abide in my love," but He also showed us how: "Even as I have kept my Father's commandments, and abide in his love."

Think what it cost Him to "keep his Father's commandments"! For the Father's will was that He should die. That He should "lay down his life for his friends." Jesus "kept that commandment" to the full, to the painful bloody end.

"Continue in my love." And the storms of life will not matter so much as we abide in the warmth of Christ's love.

Day 9

Sore Amazed

"**Oh, I'm so** glad you came," said Theresa. Tears fell down her face as she welcomed Leona and Thomas, who was a minister. "Lester is asleep just now, but he'll be glad to see you."

"We won't wake him," Thomas said quickly. "With what he's facing, he surely needs his sleep."

"All right, we'll let him sleep for a bit longer," Theresa agreed. "Please take chairs."

Quietly they discussed Lester's upcoming operation. In two days he was booked for surgery to remove a brain tumor.

"I'm having a hard time," Theresa admitted, twisting her hands in anguish. "I hadn't thought I would be so troubled. To tell you the truth, I'm ashamed of myself for being so weak."

Thomas shook his head slowly. "It is no sin to be troubled." He leafed through his New Testament. "See here, in Mark 14:33, how Jesus reacted to His coming crucifixion. It says He was 'sore amazed'. Jesus was God's Son, and He had known from eternity that He would die on the cross. Yet Jesus was also human. When it came right to the point, He was amazed, overwhelmed, by what He faced."

The room fell silent. In a choked voice Theresa admitted, "That's where my husband and I are—right to the point. We'd like to escape, but we can't. There's no way around it. Lester has to go through with this."

Quoting from Hebrews, Thomas murmured, "'We have not an high priest that cannot be touched with the feeling of our infirmities.'"

Then he went on, "It's okay to make comparisons between our reaction to suffering and Christ's reaction to suffering. But they are not the same. The difference can be illustrated using two glasses of water. The water in the one glass is perfectly clean. When we stir it with a spoon, it stays clear. That's Jesus. We could say He was agitated—His emotions were stirred—by His sufferings; but He was without sin, so there was no bitterness or despair in His suffering.

"We're like the second glass of water. At the bottom we see a brown sediment. That's our fallen nature, our inherited corruption. Agitated by sorrow, it's so easy for us to experience bitterness, discouragement, and other wrong feelings," Thomas explained.

"How true," agreed Theresa.

"By His grace, through faith," Thomas added softly, "we can overcome wrong feelings. God's strength is made perfect in weakness."

Day 10

Because Jesus Had a Mother

SANDRA WAS GOING by her friend Lisa's place and decided, on impulse, to drop in. They sat on the porch and chatted, as women will, about their families and their gardens.

Along came Sarah, their eight-year-old daughter. Waiting for a break in the conversation, she began, "Mom?"

Only it wasn't just a quick, one-syllable word like that. You know how children will give that term "Mom" an endearing, three-syllable, almost musical inflection? Like this: Mo-o-om? (Of course, in the German dialect it's Ma-a-am.)

Mother and daughter locked eyes and shared a smile. "Yes, Sarah?" said Lisa, and the eight-year-old launched into a rambling question about whether kittens can hear and whether they are afraid of thunder.

Sandra sat and listened and smiled. And smiled. Oh, the music of hearing Sarah call Lisa Mo-o-om like that!

Why so special? Because Lisa hadn't been Sarah's mom for very long. She'd been married to Sarah's dad for only seven months. Don't you think it was music to Lisa's ears to hear Sarah trustingly call her Mo-o-om—when so recently the child had the heart-pain of seeing her first mom lowered into a grave?

And if this is such music to the ears of an earthly parent, how much more does God love it when His children beseechingly call upon Him as Father? In a sense, He is not our first spiritual parent either. Paul says in Ephesians 2 that we were first "children of disobedience" and "children of wrath." Then—oh, listen to these wondrous words from Galatians: "But when the fullness of the time was come, God sent forth his Son, made of a woman, made under the law, To redeem them that were under the law, that we might receive the adoption of sons. And because ye are sons, God hath sent forth the Spirit of his Son into your hearts, crying, Abba, Father" (Gal. 4:4-6).

Did you catch that? There's an extra-special little message in there for us mothers. God's Son was "made of a woman." It's because Jesus had a mother that we may have God as our heavenly Father.

Day 11

Thy Light Is Come

Groggily Martha opened one eye and peered at the alarm clock. Time to get up—already. It seemed like such a short time ago that she'd laid her head on the pillow last night. The nights seemed shorter when she needed to get up two or three times and care for a baby.

Martha sighed and turned over. She didn't really want to face that stack of boxes, not yet unpacked, occupying one corner of the bedroom. Nor the disarray in the kitchen, evidence of having just moved into this house. It would be easier to stay in bed.

But her husband was up. She could hear him in the kitchen. Suddenly he came and said, "Quick, you must come and see the sunrise."

Minutes later Martha stood with him in the cool dawn. Their new home was in a valley; this morning it still lay in shadows.

But oh! the glory on the ridges! To the east, the sun was not yet visible, but the sky was ablaze with golden light. And to the west, the forested ramparts seemed aflame as they caught the sun's first rays. It was breathtaking.

"'Arise, shine; for thy light is come, and the glory of the Lord is risen upon thee,'" her husband began quoting from Isaiah 60:1.

Then they went inside and looked it up, and found a picture in the next verse coinciding exactly with their valley still in darkness, yet rimmed with light: "For, behold, the darkness shall cover the earth, and gross darkness the people: but the Lord shall arise upon thee, and his glory shall be seen upon thee."

Her husband found some more verses in Isaiah 52:1&2 that made Martha's face grow hot, for she thought she saw her own reluctant self tardily leaving her bed. "'Awake, awake; put on thy strength… Shake thyself from the dust… loose thyself from the bands of thy neck, O captive daughter of Zion.'"

But he was looking far beyond his sleepy wife. "Our dark valley—that's the world," he said. "And the sun is Jesus, the 'sun of righteousness', risen 'with healing in his wings.' We can't see Him. But we can see His reflected glory, shining from the church, the 'city that is set on an hill.'" And Martha saw again the reflected glory of the sunrise on the forests to the west.

So they knelt and prayed that they could truly "shake themselves from the dust" and "bear witness of that Light"—the "true Light, which lighteth every man that cometh into the world" (Jn. 1:9).

Oh, that we may all behold His glory—the "glory of the only begotten of the Father" (Jn. 1:14). May it not be for us as it was in the days of John the Baptist: "And the light shineth in darkness; and the darkness comprehended it not" (Jn. 1:5). Instead, may all the dark valley, too, become flooded with light.

Dew Drops {TWO}

Day 12

The Proper Mortar

House-building can be a long, tedious chore. Sam and Lena found that out firsthand. Here they were, taking over the home farm and doing chores twice daily, yet having to live more than a mile away while their house was being built. How tired they grew of having to travel back and forth from their rented house to milk cows on the farm, while the building project seemed to progress at a snail's pace!

It seemed there were so many little snags and obstacles that slowed the building. They'd hired their good friend Tom for the job; he was a jack-of-all-trades who would do practically everything from excavating to plumbing to landscaping. Along the way, however, he took sick not once, but three times, while the house-building waited.

Finally the rooms were ready for drywall. Sam ordered the panels, and they were promptly delivered. Tom got to work hanging the drywall, while Sam helped as much as he could in between farm work.

On the second morning of drywalling, Tom appeared apologetically on Sam's doorstep. "You're not going to believe this—but the company's recalling the drywall. There was a production problem. The drywall they delivered is sub-grade, flawed."

"You mean they'll pick up what they brought us and bring replacements?" Sam wanted to know.

Tom nodded, his eyes on the ground. "But it'll be two weeks before they can bring the better panels."

Sam nearly lost his cool. "Couldn't we just use the sub-grade stuff?" And Lena chimed in from behind him, "Surely it can't be that bad."

Tom shook his head slowly. "You'll be sorry if you do. Your walls won't last."

Caring for young children can seem like a long, slow process too. There are many trials to face. But we cannot hurry the process. We must take the time to do it right. Like the painstaking construction of a brick wall, we must teach our little children "precept upon precept" and "line upon line"(Isa. 28:13).

Above all, we must use the right materials. We dare not be like the false prophets of Ezekiel 13, who built a wall with untempered mortar. The stones were there, and they seemed to be cemented together—but the mortar failed the test.

"Therefore thus saith the Lord," cries Ezekiel, "I will even rend it with a stormy wind in my fury… So will I break down the wall that ye have daubed with untempered mortar" (Ezek. 13:13&19).

And what is the proper mortar? we mothers may well ask. Why, it is love—the love of God, the "bond of perfectness" (Col. 3:14).

Day 13

What Is the World?

Julie came skipping home from school, eager to tell Mother about her day. Inside the door she stopped short, heart plummeting. "What is it, Mother? What's wrong?" she quavered, going over to Mother, who sat pale faced in the rocking chair.

Mother raised troubled eyes. "I got a letter from my sister. Your aunt Eva."

Julie hadn't noticed the paper in Mother's hand. "What does it say? Is it something sad?"

"Yes," replied Mother. "It is indeed very sad. Remember your cousin Ben? He was here with Uncle James and Aunt Eva two years ago."

Julie's blonde pigtails bobbed up and down. "Yes, I remember Ben. He was 16, I think. And very big."

"Mmhm, Ben is tall," Mother agreed. "But now he has made his parents very sad. He has left home and gone out into the world."

"Oh," said Julie, struggling to understand what she meant. That very day at school, they had studied a map of the world. They had learned about the continents and oceans. "Doesn't everybody live in the world?" she asked

Dew Drops {two}

finally.

Mother smiled. "Yes, we all live on the earth. When I say that Ben has gone out into the world, I mean he has turned his back on the church and now chooses to live in disobedience to God."

What is the "world?" In His special petition to the Father, Jesus pleads thus for His loved ones: "I pray not that thou shouldest take them out of the world, but that thou shouldest keep them from the evil. They are not of the world, even as I am not of the world" (Jn. 17:15&16).

Again we could ask, How should we define "the world"? John lists three of the world's offspring in 1 Jn 2:16: First, "the lust of the flesh." Second, "the lust of the eyes." Third, "the pride of life." He declares, "For all that is in the world… is not of the Father, but is of the world."

Now if we reverse that statement, we have a fairly thorough definition of "the world." If it is true that all that is in the world is not of the Father, then it must be true that all that does not come from the Father is of the world. Either we are "of the Father" in Christ or we are "of the world."

The world is in collision with Christ. Everything the world prizes—its methods of pleasure, its views and use of power, its attitude towards God—is poles apart from Christ. Oh, may the prayer of Jesus be true of us: "They are not of the world, even as I am not of the world."

Day 14

All Mine Are Thine

School was out, and Molly breezed home, glad to be back after a term of teaching out-of-state. As is natural when you haven't seen a person for months, the entire family made a fuss over Molly. Mother prepared an extra-special supper the first evening she was home. In the ensuing days, Molly continued to get the lion's share of attention. Her brothers asked question after question about life in Michigan.

But a mother's heart is in tune with all her children. Noticing that 15-year-old Miriam was very subdued, Mother inquired what was troubling her. Miriam smiled sheepishly. "You know, I'm ashamed of myself. I think maybe I'm struggling because of all the attention Molly's getting. Nobody notices me that much."

"I'm sorry you had to feel that way," Mother told her. "Every one of our children is equally special. It's just—you are always here with us and we have the privilege of enjoying each other every day."

"Son, thou art ever with me, and all that I have is thine," said the father in Christ's parable, gently rebuking the prodigal's elder brother. It seemed he needed to be reminded what riches he had every day, simply because he lived always in the father's house.

Jesus didn't need to be reminded. He fully comprehended what riches were His as God's Son. "All mine are thine," He said to the Father in His prayer, "and thine are mine" (Jn.17:10). And because Jesus used nearly the same words here as in the parable of the prodigal son, we are startled to realize this truth: We too may lay claim to these words! All that the Father has promised is ours in Christ. "For all things are yours," declares the apostle. "And ye are Christ's, and Christ is God's" (1 Cor.3:21&23).

Then oh, let us truly and gratefully live as children in the Father's house, daily partaking of His riches and recognizing that we are one with all who believe. Let us lay down our all at His feet, echoing again the words of Jesus, "All mine are thine." Nothing we have is our own; it is God's, to be used to His glory, because all that He has is ours.

Day 15

Called to Be Saints

"**Mrs. Trent was** very talkative today," announced Betty upon coming home from her job helping a neighbor lady with her lawn and garden. "Talkative and happy. She kept mentioning this new saint that they have now."

Mother fixed a puzzled stare upon 17-year-old Betty's face. "Saint? Oh, I guess the Trents are Catholic."

"Yes. And Mother, it sounded so strange. This new saint is some pope—I think his name was John Paul—who's been dead for some years, and now he's been made a saint, which means people can pray to him. As nearly as I could figure out, they believe a man may be called a saint if he has worked miracles since his death." Betty shook her head slowly and repeated, "Totally, totally strange."

"Indeed so," Mother agreed seriously. "We must ask Dad about this; but I believe the Scriptures say that everyone who believes in Jesus is a saint. Sainthood is not some grand honor bestowed upon a few special people after they're dead—it's something living and real right now to us."

Dew Drops {TWO}

Paul put it briefly into words at the beginning of his letter to the Corinthians: "…to them that are sanctified in Christ Jesus, called to be saints…" In those two compact phrases we can glimpse the two aspects of sainthood.

The first is almost too marvelous for us to grasp. Because we believe, we are sanctified—made saints—in Christ Jesus. This is God's work. "Ye are washed…ye are sanctified…ye are justified in the name of the Lord Jesus, and by the Spirit of our God," declares Paul in 1 Cor. 6:11. Peter puts it this way: "Elect according to the foreknowledge of God the Father, through sanctification of the Spirit…" (1 Peter 1:2). Consecrated in Christ Jesus! We shall never cease to marvel at the wonder, that such poor sinners receive this standing simply by faith.

The second part of sainthood is more practical and everyday, though equally impossible without God. We are "called to be saints"—the Greek word here is *hagios*, which means to be holy. This is our life's work, expressed thus by Peter: "But as he which hath called you is holy, so be ye holy in all manner of conversation; Because it is written, Be ye holy; for I am holy" (1 Peter 1:15&16).

Day 16

Petitions at the Throne

How they anguished over their son's rebellious ways! Elmer and Reta could only guess at the turmoil in Ray's heart. They knew he was not at peace. They knew he was bound by wrong habits and dabbling in worldly pleasures. Time and again, they approached him to admonish and to hold out a better way, but time and again, Ray turned a deaf ear to his parents.

As never before, Elmer and Reta identified with that widow who, in a parable of Christ's, persistently appealed for justice even though the judge ignored her. She simply didn't give up until the judge hearkened to her request. Of course Elmer and Reta knew God was not like that judge; He is full of love and mercy; but they also knew He wants His children to have faith and to bring their anguished petitions to Him in constant prayer.

Back in 483 BC it was a young Jewish queen and her cousin who were in agony because they feared for their people, the Jews who lived in Persia. Haman, a man who hated the Jews, had hatched a plot to exterminate them from Persia.

What could Esther and Mordecai do to prevent Haman from killing all the Jews? True, Esther was wife to the king of Persia. But even the queen had very little influence with this powerful king. She was not even allowed to come into his presence unless he invited her.

Esther and Mordecai had faith in God. They believed He was in control, but they also believed that He would not save the Jews unless someone was willing to act on their behalf. Someone would have to risk all in order to petition the throne. And that someone was none other than Esther. She was willing to risk everything—her wealth, her position, her very life—to save her people. She sent word to Mordecai, "And so will I go in unto the king, which is not according to the law: and if I perish, I perish."

Did she not tremble as she approached that august throne? What if the king did not extend his royal scepter to show his favor? Ah, but he did—and Esther reached out a trembling hand to touch its tip.

How different it is for us when we come to the throne of God with our petitions! Esther came to a proud, imperious man; we come to the God of love and grace. Esther was not invited; we are, for the Spirit says, Come. She had a law against her; we have many promises in our favor. "Ask, and it shall be given you," promised the Lord. Esther had no one to intercede, but we have an Advocate with whom the Father is well pleased. "Let us therefore come boldly unto the throne of grace, that we may obtain mercy, and find grace to help in time of need" (Heb.4:16).

Day 17

Rejoice

Teacher Laura's chalk tapped across the blackboard. Turning to the class, she asked, "What kind of sentence is that?"

RUN TO THE BARN. One glance at the sentence, and six hands went up. "Command," came the answer.

"Okay. Now what is the subject of this command sentence?" Laura continued.

This time the hands did not go up so fast. Finally one boy offered, "Run?"

"No. RUN is a verb. The subject of a sentence is always a noun. Imagine that you are giving this command to a friend: RUN TO THE BARN. The person who gets the command is the subject of the sentence," explained the teacher.

One of the girls objected, "But the sentence doesn't say who is getting the command."

Laura smiled. "That's just it. Sentences like this have a hidden subject. So we have to supply one: YOU RUN TO THE BARN. It always works. When your mother says, 'Put on your boots,' she could have pointed a finger and said 'YOU put on your boots.'"

Smiles lit the pupils' faces. The point had come across.

In the New Testament there are not a great many such imperative sentences, where "you is only implied and the first word is a verb. But the Apostle Paul uses one such sentence, not once but four times, to let us know what we as believers in the Lord Jesus should be doing. What is the verb of this sentence? Does Paul enjoin us to "Work for the Lord"? Does he command us to "Live for the Lord"? Or might it be "Obey the Lord"?

No, it is none of those verbs. The verb is REJOICE. "Rejoice in the Lord! Rejoice evermore! Rejoice in the Lord alway! And again I say, Rejoice!"

Since the subject is implied, you and I know that Paul is pointing at us. You and I are to rejoice in the Lord. In a sense it is not a command, but a reminder of a great privilege we believers have.

Not that Paul limits his exhortations for rejoicing only to imperative sentences without subjects. Like a golden thread, the Christians' rejoicing runs throughout the apostle's writings, and through that of others as well. Peter speaks of rejoicing with joy unspeakable. And the Psalms! They overflow with injunctions to rejoice in the Lord.

Is not this food for thought? Rejoicing is pressed upon us more than working and obeying and striving. This is not to say that we do not yield ourselves in obedience as glad instruments into the hands of the Master. What it does say is that our rejoicing in the Lord comes first and foremost. All else—the struggle, the suffering, the submission—is encompassed within the golden globe of "REJOICE IN THE LORD." What rest and freedom this brings!

DAY 18

Different Kinds of Seeing

TEACHER BETTY'S STUDENTS appeared rather apathetic as she introduced the concept of osmosis during a science class. Though Betty managed to sound enthusiastic as she explained the meaning of this strange new term, most of the eyes fixed upon her stayed glazed with disinterest. The children were using their eyes, but they weren't really seeing.

"Today we're going to do an experiment to prove that plants get their nutrition through the process of osmosis," Betty announced. "Here I have a big potato, cut in half and hollowed out."

A few sparks of interest lit some of the pupils' eyes. They followed Betty's movements as she "planted" the potato in a container of water she'd colored with blue dye. Understanding began to glimmer as Betty poured a different solution—sugar water—into the potato.

But it wasn't until the following day that the students really saw for themselves what osmosis is. With cries of, "Now I see! Now I understand!" they clustered around the potato, whose hollow center had turned a vivid blue.

On the morning of Christ's resurrection, Mary, John, and Peter were also using their eyes: the words "saw" and "see" are employed four times in the *King James Version* of John 20:1-8. But did you know that the Greek actually has more than one word for different kinds of seeing?

In verse 1, Mary "seeth the stone taken away." Here the Greek word is *blepo*, which means the ordinary process of seeing with the eyes. In verse 5, the same Greek word is used when John "stooped and saw the linen clothes lying."

But in verse 6, when Peter "went into the sepulchre and seeth the linen clothes lie," we have a different Greek word: *theoreo*. This suggests far more than mere seeing. It means that Peter looked critically and carefully. I would have liked to see Peter's face just then—wouldn't you? But the Bible doesn't tell us what effect Peter's *theoreo* seeing had upon him.

Finally, in verse 8, John too entered the sepulchre, "and he saw, and believed." Here the Greek word is entirely different: *eido*. It refers to the use of the eyes, yes; but it also conveys the idea of apprehension and understanding.

What did John see? He saw and understood that no one stealing the body would have left the graveclothes carefully folded like that. He saw that Christ must indeed be risen.

Then let us not be like the people Jesus spoke of in Matt.13:13, who "seeing see not." Let us be like John, who saw—and understood—and believed.

Dew Drops {TWO}

Day 19

Pictures from the Eclipse

A partial eclipse of the moon found the whole family bundled up against the autumn chill, clustered on the back lawn and staring up at the sky. Excitement mounted as the edge of the moon turned ragged. Slowly but surely, a definite round shadow took a bite from its gleaming face.

Hearing a commotion on the other side of the hedge, Linda exclaimed, "I wonder if the Johnsons have their telescope out! May I go over and see?" With her parents' permission, she slipped through the hedge to the neighbors.

After 15 minutes she was back, saying breathlessly, "I've never seen the moon so clearly. That was spectacular, looking through the telescope. Do you know what Mr. Johnson said? The shadow of an eclipse actually makes it easier to see some features of the moon."

In Hebrews 10, the writer calls the ceremonial law "a shadow of good things to come." The law is like the shadow of an eclipse across the full glory of Christ's coming. The Hebrews writer turns his spiritual telescope upon that "shadow," focusing on the first chapters of Leviticus, where the burnt offerings and sin offerings are described.

What beautiful pictures of Christ we are shown! In Leviticus 1 we see Christ the burnt offering; He voluntarily gave His body for the sins of the world. In Leviticus 2 Christ is the meal offering, as fine flour of the best quality, anointed with the oil of the Holy Spirit, a fragrant incense to the Father. In Leviticus 3 Christ is the peace offering. He stands between God and man. And finally, in Leviticus 4 we have Christ the sin offering—He suffered outside the gate to make atonement and sanctify the people with His blood.

Now let's swing the telescope back to Hebrews 10. There in verses 5-10 we find the master key unlocking the mystery of Christ's sacrifice. First, in verses 5-8 are those words from Psalms revealing a startling fact: God did not really desire those endless, imperfect offerings of beasts upon the altar. What He desires—and what Christ provided—is poignantly described in verses 9&10: "Then said he, Lo, I come to do thy will, O God… By the which will we are sanctified through the offering of the body of Jesus Christ once for all."

"Lo, I come to do thy will." At last our lens has focused on the key, the essence of what Christ did for us. It was not so much Christ's outward anguish and bloodshedding that made reconciliation possible. It was His cry of, "Not my will, but thine, be done!" By Christ's will—fully surrendered to God—we are sanctified through His offering.

Then how gladly shall we too in full surrender "present our bodies a living sacrifice, holy, acceptable unto God…" our reasonable service, because Christ has done it first and fully for us.

Day 20

He Knew the Cost

The receptionist beckoned from the doorway. "Mr. and Mrs. Yoder, we'll see you next."

John and Amanda, along with their twelve-year-old daughter, Luella, entered the consultation room. For some reason it was dimly lit; the only light glared upon the silicone mold of Luella's teeth sitting on the center of the table.

"Hello. I'm Helen Smith, and I'm here to explain what we need to do in order to straighten Luella's teeth," began the lady behind the table.

Amanda's knees felt shaky as she took her seat. Even her unpracticed eyes could see, from that mold, what a mess Luella's teeth were. None of them lined up! What would Luella have to endure to get them straightened?

Helen picked up the mold and expertly pointed out the major faults. Then she outlined how a set of braces would align the teeth properly. Beside her, Amanda sensed a shiver going through Luella's frame. This would not be a pleasant ordeal.

John cleared his throat. Almost before Helen had concluded her presentation, he asked, "What would all this cost?"

Helen answered quietly, as if hoping to soften the blow: "Six thousand dollars."

Did John flinch? Amanda wasn't sure. She understood how he felt. Now they knew the cost—in dollars. But what about the pain and discomfort Luella would suffer? How great would that cost be?

In life, we often desire to know what something will cost. Just as often, we cannot really know ahead of time. We simply need to slog through and find out, one step or one dollar at a time.

There is an old German song that can be loosely translated thus:
Though I sought from my youth
To follow this pathway,
Yet because I was young
I often fell,
Since I did not clearly realize
That entering God's kingdom
Would cost the pain of the cross
From youth until death.

Yes, it is hard for us to grasp the full cost of the Christian life. But Jesus knew what the cost to Him would be, there in Gethsemane. Because He was God's Son, He realized ahead of time what physical and mental anguish He would suffer in order to save the world from sin. No wonder His sweat flowed as blood!

In one sense we humans cannot fully know the cost to us. Yet in another sense it is as clear-cut as the dollar figure quoted by Helen Smith. Death to the flesh. That is the price we pay for the priceless treasure of eternal life.

Day 21

Not All Was Told

An exclamation of surprise escaped Joanna's lips as she read the letter. "It's from the committee that's planning the teachers' meetings, and they want me to present a science topic."

Mother smiled. "That should be interesting. You like science."

"Well, yes, but I don't know if I can do it," Joanna hedged. However, she proceeded to throw herself into the assignment with characteristic zest.

First she decided on a topic. Then she made a foray to the library in town, copying pages of information. That was followed by a series of phone calls to some experts. Finally, on the weekend when Joanna planned to actually sit down and compose her lecture, she brought a dozen or so books home from school.

"I'd say you're well fortified," Mother commented wryly.

"I have to be," came Joanna's serious reply. "I have to present all there is to be known about my topic. Else how will it be creditable when I present it?"

Not so the writers of the Gospels. I marvel at the comments with which

John brings his account to a close. Twice—in the second-last and in the last chapter—he uses words to help us realize that "the half has not been told." In John 20:30 he says, "And many other signs truly did Jesus in the presence of his disciples, which are not written in this book." Then at the very end of the 21st chapter he reiterates, "And there are also many other things which Jesus did, the which, if they should be written every one, I suppose that even the world itself could not contain the books that should be written."

We need not ask why not more was written. Yes, if the Bible were a mere human composition, it could have been stuffed with endless stories to prove a point. If it had been written for the entertainment of the curious, it might have been more copious.

But the Gospels are neither a human effort at producing all the evidence, nor are they intended for entertainment. Listen to John's sublime presentation of the Gospels' purpose: "But these are written, that ye might believe that Jesus is the Christ, the Son of God; and that believing ye might have life through his name."

That is why the inspired penmen wrote with such noble security. They knew that the well from which they drew was limitless; but they also knew that they need not write it all. For behind their words stands an Author able to give two things that humans can never give: faith and life.

Day 22

At Thy Word

"**I'm ashamed of** myself, Mother, but…sometimes I just wish I wouldn't have to be a preacher's daughter," admitted 15-year-old Martha, her eyes downcast.

Mother was not shocked. After all, she knew what it was like to be the preacher's wife. "Tell me why," she invited quietly.

A red blush rose to the roots of Martha's hair. "I guess I wish it wouldn't always have to be my father who gets up and—and steps on people's toes and maybe embarrasses somebody." Her words ended in a sob. "I'm sorry, Mom. I didn't want to make you feel badly."

Mother waited. Once she realized Martha wasn't going to say more, she told her, "I understand how you feel. But I trust God is making good use of Dad's talent for being straightforward. And one thing that has helped both Dad and me many times is to remember this: God asked him to preach. It's not that Dad wanted the job. It's not that he can do it in his own strength. But Dad is willing to give himself up and let God use him—because God told him to."

"Thanks, Mom," Martha said humbly. "I needed the reminder."

Simon Peter must have been astonished when, after a session of preaching from the boat, Jesus turned to him and ordered, "Launch out into the deep, and let down your nets for a draught" (Luke 5:4). After all, daytime fishing was never a good idea. And besides, these waters didn't have many fish. Hadn't Peter just proved it by fishing unsuccessfully all last night?

Yes, Peter could have rejected Christ's command as too absurd. What would people think, anyway? But no, that was not Peter's reaction. This is how he responded: "Nevertheless, at thy word I will let down the net."

Charles Spurgeon, a preacher, relates how a brother once said to him, "You preach the gospel to dead sinners: you bid them repent and believe. You might as well shake a handkerchief over a grave and bid the corpse come out."

Spurgeon's response? "Exactly so. But then, I would delight to go and shake a handkerchief over graves and bid the dead live if Jesus bade me do so."

"At thy word." This is the way for all of us to serve God—whether we are preachers, teachers, parents, or servants. No matter if the tasks Jesus gives us seem thankless or embarrassing or even absurd. May we never serve the Lord simply as a matter of routine, or in our own strength. We are under God's orders! We are doing the bidding of His Word!

Day 23

The Way of His Will

"**Harold, please come** here," called Mother, putting down her hoe. "I want you to watch Benny while I go inside for a few minutes."

"Okay, Mother," the four-year-old responded agreeably, leaving the sandbox and coming to the garden. Small for his age, Harold didn't weigh a great deal more than the chubby two-year-old brother he was asked to watch.

But Mother knew she could depend on him. "I'll be indoors for about ten minutes. Make sure Benny doesn't go to the sheep pasture," she instructed.

Fifteen minutes later she left the house to the tune of shrill screams. There by the sheep pasture fence was Benny, halfway under the wire in a bid to reach those woolly creatures. But hanging desperately to his waistband was Harold, equally determined to prevent him!

Mother acted swiftly, first administering a rebuke to Benny. Then she turned to Harold. "I'm glad you held Benny back."

"Well, you said I should," he responded simply.

Mother folded the four-year-old into a hug. He had chosen the way of obedience, even though it cost him quite a struggle.

Let's turn our eyes thousands of miles away and nearly two thousand years into the past. There in the darkness we see huge waves heaving the surface of a small lake named Galilee. Toiling into the teeth of the wind is a tiny boat, its rowers nearly exhausted. The Greek version of Mark 6:48 could be rendered, "…and they were tormented in rowing, for the wind was contrary to them."

Why don't they just give up, those weary rowers, and turn back to the other shore? Riding those waves away from the wind would be so much easier.

But they want to obey their Master, whose orders were thus: "…he constrained his disciples to get into the ship, and to go to the other side…" (Mark 6:45). The disciples chose the way of His will, regardless what it cost them.

The way of His will! May we never choose another way, even when we see that the way of His will may be the way of the storm. And as we choose the path of obedience, we will discover the same sublime truth that the disciples did: the way of Christ's will is also the way of His power. No storm can make His almighty footsteps falter. No waves are a deterrent to Him. And when He enters the ship, the storm itself succumbs to His power and is still.

Day 24

Part 1: Doubts Can Have a Purpose

"**Mother, I feel** so miserable," sighed Katie one Monday afternoon as she ironed her brother's shirts.

"Why, Katie?" Mother asked gently.

The teenager replied, "I guess it's mostly my doubts that are causing the problems."

"Doubts about what?" came Mother's next question.

"Oh, so many things. And it torments me, because I know it's wrong. Christians shouldn't be doubting. They should have faith and assurance!" Katie's voice changed to a wail.

Mother's heart agonized along with her daughter. She remembered what it was like to be new in the faith. "Katie," she said, "just having some doubts is not necessarily sinful. It's when doubts turn to stubbornness—and stubbornness becomes a lifestyle—that we are in trouble."

"Oh," breathed Katie. "Well, I hope I'm not being stubborn. But still, why can't I be more stable? Why all these doubts?"

"I'm glad you're opening up about this," Mother told her warmly. "Tonight when Dad gets home, we'll have a chat with him. Then I hope you

Dew Drops {two}

honestly express your doubts. Silent doubts rarely get answers."

Katie smiled. "Answers are what I need, all right."

Mother agreed, "That's just it. If doubts lead to questions—and questions lead to answers—and the answers are accepted—then doubt has done a good work."

Thomas was an honest doubter. When he openly expressed his vexing doubts, Jesus wasn't hard on him. What sublime patience we see in Christ's treatment of this weak disciple! He did not scold Thomas outright, though we see loving rebuke in the way He commanded Thomas, word for word, to do as He had said he must in order to believe: "Reach hither thy finger, and behold my hands; and reach hither thy hand, and thrust it into my side: and be not faithless, but believing."

Thomas may have been surprised that Jesus knew about the declaration of doubt he'd made the week before. But really, we shouldn't be amazed. Never a doubt crosses our mind that Jesus doesn't know it.

Can we fathom the Lord's love for Thomas—so great that He invited the disciple to touch His open wounds? Yet is His love any less towards us today? Then let us be like Thomas, not staying mired in our doubts, but letting the love of Jesus draw us onward to faith.

Day 25

Part 2: The Substance

"Mother says you're troubled with doubts," Father began kindly when he and Mother and Katie were together that evening.

Katie twisted her hands in her lap. "Yes. I'm ashamed of those doubts. But I keep wondering—how can I know that I'm a Christian? How can Jesus accept me if I fall so often?"

Father was silent. "Those are honest questions. I want to ask you another: are you looking in the right place for answers?"

"Uh—I'm not sure what you mean," Katie admitted, sounding a little startled.

"Well, as long as we look at ourselves for answers, focusing on our failures, it's no wonder our footing is unsure. Let me ask you another question that will help you take a complete turn and look away from yourself: Katie, do you believe that God is who He says He is? In other words, that He is almighty God?"

The question had the desired effect. Katie's eyes lit up and she answered sincerely, "Yes, I do."

"And do you," Father went on swiftly, "believe that He does what He says?

That God fulfills His promises?"

"Yes," came her reply, just as freely as the first.

"Then that can take care of doubts. God is God; He sent His Son to save us; and Paul writes to the Philippians, 'Being confident of this very thing, that he which hath begun a good work in you will perform [complete] it until the day of Jesus Christ'" (Phil.1:6).

"It's like a solid footing to stand on," Mother commented with a smile.

One writer has said, "Doubt was never meant to be a permanent condition. Doubt is one foot lifted, poised to step confidently when the footing is found."

"Faith is the substance of things hoped for," says the Hebrews writer. The word translated "substance" is *hypostasis* in Greek, which signifies "subsistence," a foundation for another thing to stand on. In a sense, then, "faith" is our foundation.

In another sense, Jesus Christ the Son of God is Himself our great Foundation and Cornerstone. Did not the hesitant, doubting foot of Thomas come down in a swift, sure step when he cried out in newfound faith: "My Lord and my God." Faith is just as Katie's father put it: believing that God is God, and that He does as He says. "Faithful is he that calleth you, who also will do it" (1 Thess. 5:24).

Day 26

Family Affection

Ben and Brenda hadn't realized what it would be like to become grandparents. Over the years, of course, they'd seen how their friends made much of their grandchildren. But it wasn't until Ben and Brenda's first grandchild was born that the full impact hit them.

"I can't see enough of little Timothy," Brenda confessed to Ben. "I'd like to go over to Adams every day, just to cuddle Timothy. Every time I see him at church, I get this powerful urge to hold him."

Ben smiled. "It's almost like having a baby of our own again."

Almost. But not quite. Is there anything on earth to compare with a mother's affection for her child? The bond is so tender, so true, so deep, so strong, that no other earthly affection rivals it.

Did you know that's precisely the kind of affection Paul was referring to in Romans 12:10? In fact, he mentions two kinds of affection in a single verse. Here's the verse, with several of the words in the original Greek: "Be *philostorgos* one to another with *philadelphia*; in honor preferring one another."

That last Greek word sounds like a city in Pennsylvania, doesn't it? It's no accident. William Penn knew his Greek when he founded the "city of brotherly love."

So that defines *philadelphia*: it means brotherly love. We're one family in Christ, loving one another as brothers.

But what about *philostorgos*? It seems the Greeks had a word for everything—especially for the different kinds of human affection! Where we have to use three or four words, they had a single term.

Take, for instance, love of money. That's *philarguria*. Or lovers of self—they're *philautos*. Then there's *philedonos*, lovers of pleasure. Or how about *philoxenos*, lover of hospitality?

To get back to the particular affection we're talking about: the Greek word *philostorgos* means the special, tender affection that parents have for their children.

"Be kindly affectioned one to another with brotherly love," the verse says in English. Now we realize it's loaded with deep meaning. Family love—brotherly love. That's the kind of love true followers of Christ have for each other! Is it any wonder, since we're actually members of one body? In a sense that's even more intimate than being members of one family.

Then the last part of the verse supplies a very pointed definition of how such love shows up in action. "In honor preferring one another." The true Christian considers his brethren more worthy than himself. He is not envious when he sees that another is made much of while he himself is neglected. That's *philostorgos* and *philadelphia*, put to work in everyday life.

Day 27

Drawn to the Fire

"Mom, maybe we should cancel our hot dog roast," Ellen suggested after a glance at the thermometer. "At the rate the mercury's dipping, it's going to be a chilly evening!"

Mom moved over to catch a glimpse of the thermometer. She agreed, "Maybe we should cancel."

But Linda spoke up quickly, "Remember, we'll have a fire. Surely it can keep us warm."

So they went on with their plans. By the time the other two families arrived, a fire was roaring and crackling in the pit. Everyone huddled close, enjoying the heat as it radiated into the chilly evening.

The night air was cold, too, on that spring day many years ago when Peter warmed himself at the servants' fire in the courtyard. "And the servants and officers stood there," writes John in chapter 18:18, "who had made a fire of coals; for it was cold: and they warmed themselves: and Peter stood with them, and warmed himself."

Ah, that fire in the courtyard! It was the site of Peter's greatest failure. Why was he there, mingling with his enemies and the enemies of his Master—while above him in the chamber Jesus was on trial? And why did Peter fail so utterly?

Three reasons come to mind. They are three reasons with which we can all identify. Have not we all failed, and was it not always due to one or more of these reasons?

1. There in the garden when his Lord was praying in agony, receiving strength for the coming ordeal—where was Peter? Asleep. Do we also at times miss out on opportunities to call on God for strength?

2. Peter was far too self-confident. "I won't forsake you even if all the others do," he had boasted. Before we can be strengthened, we must see our weakness. Our own resolution alone will not sustain us in the conflict. God's strength is "made perfect" only in weakness.

3. By mingling there with the servants and warming himself at their fire, Peter put himself in an extremely dangerous place. Remember the way the devil tempted Jesus. "God has promised to give His angels charge over thee, lest thou dash thy foot against a stone," Satan taunted. "Surely you can cast yourself from the pinnacle of the temple without harm." But Jesus would not listen to the devil even if he quoted Scripture.

So when we come near to a great temptation—when, perhaps, we are drawn to warm ourselves at the world's fires—let us ask ourselves: *Whose voice is it that bids me do this*? And if it is not definitely the Lord's, then let us run as fast as we can in the opposite direction—even if the night is cold.

Day 28

False Humility

Creak, creak, creak went the porch swing. The faster it squeaked, the faster fell the tears of the young girl sitting on the seat. No one was on the porch to see, so Jane allowed her tears to flow freely as dusk settled down around her.

But someone did see, and before long Jane heard a soft footstep. Mother sat down beside her, inquiring, "What is it, Jane?"

She dashed a hand across the tears. "I did it again. I wanted to do better today, but I failed in so many ways."

Mother was silent. She knew Jane's weaknesses, knew what mistakes were troubling her. After a while she simply quoted, "'If we confess our sins, he is faithful and just to forgive us our sins, and to cleanse us from all unrighteousness'" (1 Jn.1:9).

Jane burst out, "I wish I wouldn't have to ask for forgiveness so often!"

"God can certainly give us victory. But it is a false kind of humility if we can hardly bring ourselves to ask forgiveness when we fail," replied Mother.

Maybe Peter thought he was being humble, there in the precious final hours before the cross when Jesus donned a towel and stooped to wash His disciples' feet. In horror the impetuous apostle exclaimed, "You'll never wash my feet! Why, you're my Master—why should you serve me?"

True, Peter had a great respect for his Master. But under his show of humility and modesty was a contradiction to the will of the Lord. What Peter didn't understand was the full import of the Lord's words in Mark 10:45, "The Son of man came not to be ministered unto, but to minister, and to give his life a ransom for many."

If Peter couldn't submit simply to having his feet washed by the Master, how could he ever submit to the much deeper sacrifice Jesus was about to make—namely, giving His life for the world's sin?

No, it is not humility to refuse what the Lord wishes to do for us. Rather, it is self-willed presumption. John tells us in ch.13:5, "After that he poureth water into a basin, and began to wash the disciples' feet…" The work Christ began there at the supper table has never ended. Today He is still stooping to wash the grime of sin from our feet as we come repentantly to Him in the twilight hours of each day.

The truest humility is to receive reverentially and thankfully the gifts of grace.

Day 29

He Wanted to See

"**What is it** like inside a chimney?" wondered Nathan. "I wish I could see."

Mother smiled. This was so typical of the seven-year-old. He always wanted to see things for himself. Just being told about something was not enough; he needed to be shown.

"There's nothing to see inside a chimney," Mother assured him. "Nothing but filthy black soot, because of all the smoke that goes up."

"Hmmm, soot," mused Nathan. "I wonder what that looks like."

"Someday when I clean out the stovepipes I could show you soot," Mother offered.

But the impetuous Nathan did not want to wait for "someday." When, a few hours later, Mother heard a noise above her head, she instantly guessed what was on. She dashed outdoors. There on the roof was Nathan, peering down the chimney.

It seems Christ's disciple Philip was a little like Nathan. He wanted to see.

He wanted to be shown. Jesus had told His disciples "If ye had known me, ye should have known my Father also: and from henceforth ye know him, and have seen him" (Jn.14:7). But that was not enough for Philip. Impulsively he cried, "Lord, show us the Father, and it sufficeth us."

Obviously, Philip was picturing an Old Testament style of revelation. Wouldn't that be glorious, if God were to show Himself by thunder and lightning as in the days of old?

Philip was in error. No wonder we can detect sadness and pain in our Lord's reply: "Have I been so long with you, and yet hast thou not known me, Philip?"

Already in the first chapter of John's Gospel we find Philip declaring that Jesus is the Messiah. Yet here—after months of daily walking with Jesus—we realize that Philip still knew very little about the Lord.

Are we any different? Yes, we call Jesus our Lord and Saviour—but do we truly know Him as He is in the Father? Have we not, like Philip, still very much to learn about our precious Lord?

It is true that Philip was in error to request a literal appearing of the Father. Yet in a sense we ought all to be like Philip. The deepest yearning of our heart should be to be shown the Father—to really see God with our spiritual eyes. Why? Because Jesus says in John 17:3, "And this is life eternal, that they might know thee the only true God, and Jesus Christ whom thou hast sent." To see God is to have eternal life.

Day 30

Groan Not

The kitchen door banged open, and two red-faced youngsters burst in. "Somebody took all our glads!" exclaimed Harvey.

Helen added indignantly, "And all our money too."

Father, who was working at his desk, looked up with a puzzled air. "Your glads?"

Mother explained quickly, "They'd put some of their gladiolus flowers at the end of the driveway to sell. The stalks are 50¢ each, and people are supposed to put the money in a little box."

"Ah, yes. You did that last summer too. So somebody took your money?" questioned Father.

"Those wicked people must have stolen five dollars!" Harvey sputtered.

Father cautioned, "Let's remember to suffer patiently if we are wronged. After all, our experiences aren't much, compared to the persecution some Christians in other countries have to endure." He held up a magazine. "Here's a picture of a church that was bombed out of hatred for the believers."

The children quickly forgot their own grievance as they inspected those pictures. Soon they hurried out to pick more glads, and Father returned to his accounting.

Minutes later, he let out an impatient groan. "I see that George still hasn't paid his account. That certainly messes up my books."

Mother didn't reply right away. She knew to whom he referred; George was a brother in the church. Maybe sometime she would gently ask her husband this question: Is it right to be impatient with a brother, when we know we should exercise patience towards wrong suffered from unbelievers?

"Groan not one against another, brethren," says James in 5:9. The *KJV* actually says "grudge not," but every commentator I checked maintains that a better translation of the Greek would be "groan"—a half-suppressed murmur of impatience and harsh judgment. And James delivers this exhortation to "groan not" against the brethren right after giving a vivid description of how we should patiently suffer wrong at the hands of the wicked.

Are we not all sometimes caught by this? Why are we so impatient at offenses from the brethren? Why do we groan and shake our heads at their trivial mistakes and failings?

Also in verse 9, James has a stiff warning against such groaning: "…lest ye be condemned: behold, the judge standeth before the door." Here, commentators suggest that a better translation would be, "…lest ye be judged." To "groan against one another" is actually to judge—and this brings to mind the solemn echoes of Matt.7:1&2: "Judge not, that ye be not judged. For with what judgment ye judge, ye shall be judged—"by that august Judge who stands at the door.

Dew Drops {TWO}